graffiti in red lipstick

For my son Stuart

graffiti in red lipstick

Magi Gibson

Curly Snake Publishing

821·914

Acknowledgements

Some of these poems first appeared in
*Strange Fish, Premier Results, The Herald, Seam,
Campus, Recurring Themes, Chapman, Cencrastus,
Nerve, Cutting Teeth, Northwords, The Eildon Tree,
Skinklin Star.*

The author would like to thank the Royal Literary
Fund for the fellowship which allowed her time to
complete this collection.

The publisher acknowledges support from the Scottish
Arts Council towards the publication of this title.

Curly Snake Publishing
Cencrastus
Unit One
Abbeymount Techbase
2 Easter Road
Edinburgh
EH8 8EJ

Scottish
Arts Council

Contents

Foreword

This new volume shows an already accomplished poet developing in new directions. It demonstrates, yet again, that Magi Gibson's appeal goes far beyond the mere highbrow. These are poems which walk the streets and fields and are easily, and lovingly, greeted by all who meet them.

The feisty, satirical Wild Woman still makes her mark here; but a new, more meditative, contemplative tone is also apparent. There are longer, reflective sequences, coupled with short imagistic poems of lyrical quality and spiritual lucidity. There is also a darker seam being mined; and there are poems of deep psychological insight which can be disturbing and unsettling as well as witty and hard-hitting.

If this volume marks the beginning of a shift in the poet's work, it is one that will not lose her readers but will take them into new territories and, indeed, gain her many new admirers. Magi Gibson is not only one of the most important women writers in Scotland, but one of Scotland's best poets per se.

It was some years ago now that I wrote in Cencrastus "Blessed be Magi Gibson for the country hath need of such a voice - made in Scotland from girders". Well, the girders are expanding. There are some truly exquisite gems in this volume but, taken as whole, the collection also maps something of a personal, spiritual journey for the writer which the more reflective reader may wish to pick up on.

But it is also a book you can just dip into. On every and any page you will find images that delight, voices that amuse or make you laugh aloud, and lines that zing in your heid in the way that only the best of poetry can.

Enjoy.

Raymond Ross
At the Sign of the Curly Snake
April 2003

the poet

like a buzzard, she circles
the sky of her imagination

eye alert to the flash of white
the sudden dash

of an untamed thought

a quiet daughter

they found me in the corner
way at the back
of my mother's wardrobe

at first they thought I was a button
broken loose from a frayed thread
or a mothball, happy in the dark

then as I grew, they though I was
a shoe without a partner, but
they were busy folk – it was easier
to poke me back beside the fallen
jumpers and the missing socks

as for me, I was quite content
tucked up in the folds of mother's frocks

from time to time she'd drag me out
wear me, dangled prettily
on the end of her arm – the ultimate accessory
a quiet daughter

black heat

pit wheel
slowly turning
black-spoked giant

from the mineshaft of memory
you draw a smiling child
waiting at the pit-head gate

miner
he did not have a garden
but a plot, to grow a functional crop
carrots, leeks, potatoes

but always he kept a corner
where he cultivated flowers
to feed his soul
after a twelve hour shift
of eating into darkness

lousing time
bursting from the cage
black creatures
frightening
until they smiled
white teeth human

the miners' perk
coal castles dumped
for dirty wee rascals
to be kings on

coal
burning in the grate
wind howling in the lum
we saw castles, dungeons
fire-breathing dragons

our parents saw money
going up in smoke
and worried lest winter
last too long

bings
once they peaked like witches' hats
brooding, dark, they shadowed us
as we skipped to park and school

but today?

shrunken sugar loaf plateaux
sparkling white with last night's snow

The Pit-Owner's Wife Says

the pit owner's wife says
what you don't understand
is that miners loved mining

and I think of my grandfather
miles underground day after day
hour after hour and how he swore
none of his sons
would go down the pit

see how hard they fought
to keep their jobs, they even took
the chance to buy the pits
she says

and I think of my uncle
who followed his father
and traded his lungs
I remember his wheezing
the struggle for breath

I've been down a pit
the pit-owner's wife says
*the most **exrtorrdinary** experience*
such silence, like in a cathedral
religious really

and I think of my grandfather
down on his knees, skin black as sin
day after day, hour after hour

oh of course, the pit-owner's wife says
when you get to the coalface
where the men are working -
then there's noise. What noise!

and I think of my uncle
and how my aunt hollered
when his aid was turned off

and you know what I did, she says
six miles underground
I chiseled out my own piece
of genuine Scottish coal!

and I think of my grandfather
and the genuine
grime ingrained in his skin
and the genuine
coal dust black in his lungs
and the genuine
misery black in his heart

I treasure it, she says.
My own piece of coal.
Beautiful. Quite beautiful.

My Father's Dungarees

My father's dungarees, brown,
musty smell of putty and plaster
patched at the knees
where they're worn thin
from the supplicant toil of the slater.

But he to me was the High Priest
the Great Almighty of my youngest years
man above all others, a fine master of his trade.
In my young eyes his drab clothes glowed
fine robes to mark his sacred place
high on the roof of my small universe.
From far below I gazed, but never saw
his fears.

I never knew he wore the uniform
the working man must wear -
dank smelling dungeon clothes
of those nailed firmly down
a mark of Cain they bear
forever recognized, looked down
and despised by them, those others.

Eleven years old my small world lost its roof
when I was told the truth of who I was,
where I should remain.

Don't let her play with us, a classmate said,
Her father comes home filthy.

And so illusions of myself, my father
came tumbling down in ruins.

Eleven years old, they set me firmly
in my place where I should stay, never dream
of straying upwards, of being seen with them
teachers' and bankers' daughters.

My father's dungarees, brown
musty smell of putty and plaster
patched at the knees
by hands worn sore, worn sour.

Forty years on I know what I would say -
I'm proud to wear those dungarees today.

Miners' Daughters

Their hair is honey-blond and styled.
Their clothes are well-made, warm.
And on their fingers gold rings shine.

But in the memory of their bones
rickets lurks like an ache.

And their lungs still recall
the hacking coughs
of grandfathers they never met.

At night in the dark pit of their dreams
they are down on their knees
tunneling, chipping
at the hard black face of the future.

And even as they sit, well-groomed
picking at breakfast in this posh hotel
there is a trace of coal dust
beneath their polished fingernails.

unbarbing the candle

as the baby bird turns its gaping beak
towards the mother
as the pup, blind and wriggling, seeks
the sweet warm nipple
I turned to you

and you were a candle
flaring, golden
against the dark

only once I'd cut myself
and bled, did my eyes grow
accustomed to your brightness
only then did I see the razor wire
the bristling barbs you'd placed
between yourself and others

all through my childhood, you shone
unreachable, untouchable, beautiful
as a rose hedged in by thorns

you burned with a cold light – yet
is it not true that the heat
from a lone light bulb
or from a single candle
can save a freezing soul from death?

I hungered to come close, to know skin
on skin, soul on soul, but pain and fear
of pain stilled the hunger in me

mother, I am still your child
though child no more

and with the fingers of a woman
who knows that pain will ease
that cuts will heal, that scars well-won,
well-worn, can have a beauty of their own

with these woman's fingers
I will undo each barb
I will unwind the razor wire
I will come close to you before

your light flares and fades
in a final guttering

stone child

downstairs
her mother's voice
erupts
flows red and hot as lava
her father roars
his rage a heaving ocean

upstairs in her bed
the child lies
foetal-curled
still

as the stone child
in the ruins of Pompeii

OnceUponADream
(a multiple choice poem for little girls)

you are a
      pretty ballerina
      lonely princess
      poor little rich girl
with sugar pink cheeks and a sugar pink dress
and you wait all day in a
      music box
      castle
      windowless tower
for a handsome
      prince
      soldier
      cowherd
      knight
with muscles and magic
tucked up his sleeve
where little girls have hankies
and a sweet tooth that can't resist
your sugar pink lips
and he falls
      madly
      sweetly
      passionately
in love with you and
      sweeps
      carries
      steals
you away to his
      kingdom
      castle
      semi
      pad

and this is the dream your
       mother
       aunt
       sister
       granny
fed you with your rusks
taught you with your ABC,
your 1-2-3, read to you at bedtime and
swore was as real was as true as
       the tooth fairy
       santa claus
       the virgin mary
now every night the
       prince
       soldier
       cowherd
       king
steals into your room and
       slobbers
       slavers
       smacks
his lips/belly/thighs
when he sees you
sweet and helpless on the bed and
with a bound/a leap
he tries to
       eat
       gobble
       swallow
       consume you
and you wake screaming
thrashing and sweating and
shivering and cold
cold as a fish
waiting for the blade
to slit its belly open

you all die at fifteen, said diderot

I am fifteen, you a little older
together we swim out to the island
only water and silence between us
and I feel the loch's dark undertow
and I recall my mother's warnings
and the words of diderot

hours later, the sun low, the air
a mist of midges, we know we must go
back, and the sharp shingle pinches my feet
and I shiver, my costume not quite dry
clinging to my skin, and I
go in first, the cold
clenching
tight as my father's fist
the water rasping
harsh as my mother's tongue

breathless, jelly-legged, at last I flop
beside the folded clothes. I wrap your towel
around me, soft as your touch against my skin
and looking up I see
the island and the clump of trees
the small scree beach, the flies dancing
and a salmon leaping in a silver arc
as my heart leapt when you touched my breast
but the loch is still, the whole world empty

your name leaps from my throat, bursts
the bubble of the air, leaps again and again
a fish flailing on a hook

suddenly you're there
black hair seal-sleek
pale body glistening

later alone, I weep
for the child who swam out to the island
and did not return

advice to a younger sister

Our mother's house is booby-trapped –
don't be fooled by the sofa
soft and deep as milky breasts,
the coffee table polished to a grinning sheen,
the mirror smiling back as you come in,
the television blaring Sunday hymns.

Look closer at that reading lamp
she says is just to help her poor old eyes –
one twist and it's a bare interrogation bulb.

See, little sister, how I am summoned here
at each full moon to squirm beneath
the magnifying glass of her maternal eye.

This, I say, is my daughter
and I'm sorry, mother
she is not beautiful enough
and chooses to live unwed
with a callous, pimply youth.

And this is my career,
a sunken sorry sponge cake
that has not risen high enough.

And I know, oh mother dear,
that I have let you sadly down
with my tiny flat thick-furred with dust.

Take my advice, little sister.
Go back only if you must –
that bearskin rug outstretched
before the fire
has teeth
and they are bared at you.

psychological kick boxer

psychological kick boxer, she leaps,
flicks an agile foot, delivers a blow, so
quick, so slick, so fleet, so neat
you don't know - until you feel the pain
that you've been hit – again

*

today she is a ray of sunshine, and you,
mad dog, rush out to mid-day play,
glad that winter's through

gleeful as a soldier when a truce is called
you toss your helmet in the trench

convinced by the sweetness in her voice
you offer her the olive branch

dazzled by the radiance of her smile
you do not see the storm clouds gather

ears filled with her laughter
you do not hear the rumbling thunder

*

today is a Be-Nice-to-You-Day
you know this right away –
she's taken out her evil eye
and popped it in a box and
locked it in a drawer

inside the box the eye lies wide awake
bright as a marble, shiny as a summer sky
the evil eye can never close, never
rest or sleep or doze . . .
in the darkness of the box it starts to roll
and with its evil stare it bores
pepper-pot, pin-prick holes into your soul

*

stand. . . perfectly. . . still don't twitch
or move one hair don't blink don't talk
too loud laugh just enough a titter not a
giggle don't say too much don't say too little
don't stand too far way don't stand too near
she bobs around you an unexploded mine
inside your skull insistent as sonar bleeps
alarm bells sound your head swivels
scanning empty seas you dare not breathe
you're trapped inside you cannot leave
you are about to drown in enemy waters

*

sometimes you lie awake and wonder
why some days she's sugar, others she's shite
but most of all you wonder why
of all the people in this world
you're the one she chose to spite

*

she's like the Scottish weather -
shows just enough sunshine
so you won't emigrate to a kinder place
which in any case
would be impossible
since she holds the passport
to your heart

*

you've got it all wrong, she says
just like you – always grasping
the wrong end of the stick
when all I'm trying to do
is beat you with it

strange fish

at the beach she would not dabble in the shallows
or leap the rippling waves, instead she sat
and moaned the water was too cold

strange fish
she preferred to flounder on dry land
fretting that the sun might scorch her scaly skin

did she never long for
the soft turquoise caress of water?

did she never wish she could lie back,
freed from the dead weight of being human?

did she never feel her fish-tail twitch or itch to slip her
fingers into emerald crevices, then lick
the salt-taste from her glistening skin?

despite lessons at the pool
she never learned to swim

drowning in self-denial
was more her style

the moral policeman

I don't like women who swear, he says
eyeballing her like a minister from the pulpit.

Most unladylike, he opines. You are educated, intelligent,
attractive, well-able
to express yourself in other ways

fuck off, she says

like an amulet

today I walked right past
a gypsy selling lucky heather
and stared right through her evil eye

I carelessly strolled under a painter's ladder
I put my shoes on the table
I did not salute the magpie

I broke seven mirrors
and laughed seven times

I trod on every crack
on every slab on every pavement
and the bad witch did not suck me down

because today
I wear your love
like an amulet

I laugh in the teeth of growling dogs
I walk out alone in the dark
which, of course, is not dark
because my body shines
my eyes burn like embers

and even when I'm on my own
I'm not alone, because I wear
your love like an amulet

guitar

I envy the guitar
you cradle in your lap

I envy the guitar
smooth brown warm
cradled in your lap

I watch your fingers
sensitive to each quiver
and shudder and envy
the guitar which trembles
at your touch

come to me, I long to say
cradle me in your arms
touch the smooth brown of my body
till even my hair sings
with the beauty of it

hold me

hold me, as the wind holds me
on this mountainside
hold me tight - my body is
as light as a star
when I'm by your side

hold me close against your skin
let my fingers anchor in
the softness of your hair

explore me, as the wind explores me
– there is no rippling loch, no sheltered cave,
no wooded hill, no part of me
your tongue, your fingers
may not touch or feel

take my breath away as
the wind takes my breath away
on this mountainside

hold me, as the wind holds me,
never let me fall into the dark abyss
of loneliness

selkie runes

1

the wet sand the sea has lain on
bears imprints of weed and kelp

like your skin in the morning
marked by the tangles of my hair

2

seals at catterline
ancestors
in the tossing waves of time
watch us
as we make our way
clumsily, unsteadily
along the rocky shore

three seconds of his voice

three seconds of his voice
on the answering machine
makes her smile

for several hours
enables her to handle
the rude woman in the corner shop

with unprecedented pleasantness
gets her through a morning
at the pc screen

without once cursing
or strangling the mouse
with its umbilical cord

finds her giving a helpful hand
to the office wanker -
this is when she knows

she's lost it
totally

a perfect wife

a perfect wife has clean fingernails
keeps a clean house, makes a creaseless bed
lies in it happily, even when he doesn't

a perfect wife never answers
first/back/correctly

a perfect wife conceives at the drop of a
hat, blooms when she is with child
delivers daintily - a perfect son

a perfect wife breast-feeds discreetly
does not squirt milk when making love
feigns ignorance on premature ejaculation/
vaginal irritation and most especially
clitoral stimulation

a perfect wife is secure enough to say
I am not a feminist
in a non-confrontational fragrant feminine way.

a perfect wife is flexible, will bend
over backwards (position 252)
to please her husband.

a perfect wife smiles
when doors are opened for her
does not see doors slammed in her face
thinks the glass ceiling is
an architectural innovation

a perfect wife comes
(quietly)
in sizes ten and twelve
a perfect wife has
A PERFECT WIFE©
punched out on her back.
A PERFECT WIFE©
is a Registered Trade Mark
available only while stocks last

Mitigation

In a moment of hormonal madness
one woman shot her man
in the groin with his hunting gun

another slammed her car into
a juggernaut that jammed her way

yet another flung herself
from a ninth floor window.

I had such a moment today,
spent two hundred pounds
I did not have, on clothes
I did not need, that made me look,
frankly, like a tart. Then told
the shop assistant, yes,
I'd like to wear them right away.

You stared in disbelief
as I teetered in on 6 inch heels.
What else can I plead, but oh
it really could have been
so much worse.

Normandy War Cemetery

Twenty years after the war
a woman and a young girl kneel
beside a grave in Northern France,
its headstone white as weathered bone.

The child stands up, eyes all but blinded
by the golden medal of the sun.
She thinks of history at school,
of old war films, of aeroplanes on fire,
she thinks of heroes and of Victory

then counts the headstones
jutting from the earth, until they blur
and she begins to grasp infinity
the raw futility of war.

She leaves her mother kneeling there
carefully arranging flowers
the blooms already wilting in the heat.

From time to time she stops to read -
the story always stays the same -
a date of birth, a date of death,
a regiment, a name.

Thirty years on, grown to a woman,
she kneels where once her mother knelt,
the grass an unchanged lawn of perfect green,
the August heat still searing on her skin.

She watches as her daughter walks
by stones stark, white as weathered bone
a bitter crop - it never grows or withers
never reaches autumn.

blackbird

blackbird, outside my window
the worm wriggling in your beak
forms a living question mark
dies   asking   why

spoils of war

you would have made a whore of her
the twelve year old girl
whose body you raped
in the name of the fatherland
the twelve year old
with the tear-stained face you sold
for the price of a slap-up meal
and a flask of cheap wine
but really
you made a monster of yourself

and now you would make
a murderer of me
for if given a loaded gun
and a steady hand

how could I resist the urge
to satisfy my craving
to pump you full to pump you full
of silver bullets
deadly   hot   searing

the hunter

only kills for the table, he says

the table shifts uneasy
on its four stout legs

a shadow drifts across
its polished face

as it wonders
what will be put on it next

saboteur to hunter

I don't want to see your human face
I don't want to know your kids think
you're the best dad since sliced bread
and your wife thinks the sun shines out your arse

I don't want to meet your silver-haired mother
who's eighty now and gaga
and worships you like a golden calf
because you bring red roses every birthday

I don't want to hear about your charitable deeds
your sponsored bunjee-leaping-twelve-day-fast-
and marathon for orphans in Rumania/
kidswithleukaemia/gentlewomenindistress
and what a jolly santa claus you are Ho-Ho-Ho

No. I don't want to see your human face
just like you don't want to see
the soft eye of the doe
as she twitches in the heather
life spurting from her breast
and stares, uncomprehending
at your knife

night creatures

there are those of us
who look as dead as tree bark

who lie still and green
as a folded leaf, who

seem ancient and parched
as papyrus

then startle you with
sudden fluttering

you think you know us
name us Moth

at dusk we decorate
the dark glass of your rooms

delicate pastel petals
pale as moonbeams

as dawn breaks we grow restless
flit by your sleeping face

kiss your lips, gentle
as a breath

before you wake we slip
into your dreams, soundless
as the souls of the dead

this empty house

day one

I come back alone
dust drifts, plants thirst
petals litter the floor like sad confetti
my footfall echoes in the hall
a spider spins a web across the bedroom door

day two

the heating splutters
a pulse, a heartbeat
a welcome drone

day three

I clatter pots, pans
as if like tribal drums
their clattering might keep
your ghost at bay

day four

daybreak, the sun gapes
pink, wet, raw
in an iodine sky

day five

6 a.m. I cannot sleep. I turn
the radio on, disasters tug the drawn
blinds of my consciousness.
I wash. I dress. Alone.

10a.m. I turn the radio on.
It sings a sad love song.
I grip my coffee mug. I weep.

day six

your presence lingers in the deep red
of the ring-mark where
once your wine glass sat

day seven

your man-smell clings to covers, curtains,
duvet, pillowslips. I open all the windows wide
breathe deep

day eight

in the shower, one dark hair curling
not mine
I turn the water
hotter than I can bear

day nine

your presence haunts
every cubic inch of every room
visible/invisible
as dust in sudden sunlight

day ten

I pack each photo of your smile away
but it lives on in every cell
in every gland in every nerve

day eleven

a ghost would be easy
I'd learn to live with sudden chills
strange patterns on the walls
a creak, a thud, a crash
but the absence of you makes no noise
spooks

day twelve

in the mirror my eyes are
your eyes
you haunt this house
please leave please stay

day thirteen

I can't recall your face – just fragments,
the tiny mole upon your cheek,
the tooth you chipped when you were small,
but if I close my eyes my lips and fingertips recall
every curve, dip, inch in perfect detail

night thirteen

beside me is a space
where you once were
the space is not empty

night fourteen

in the bathroom I light candles
sing a slow song, sink back in scented water,
sip blood-red wine as shadows dance
am cleansed

night fifteen

scatter of sequins
velvet blanket of black
silver moon earth gazing

day sixteen

I drift through each day
on the dark lake of memory
behind me water ripples
in soft silken ridges -
though you are gone
the ripples of you follow me
silken, gentle as your touch

day seventeen

I begin to understand
that sunshine seen
through shattered glass
is beautiful

night seventeen

above my head stars sparkle:
though it has gone into tomorrow
the sun's wild fire fills their worthless dust
with diamond light

you too are gone, my heart is dust
and yet – I sparkle still

I just wanna be loved. . .

'women want to be wanted, not to be loved'

Mon cher monsieur Lacan
far be it from me to set
a great psychologist to rights
but I think it only fair
to let you know
that as a woman
I don't want to be *wanted*

I'm not a small ad in the local paper –
an upright baby grand, a caravan
with matching picnic table
nor am I a good home for an orphaned pup
stuck on a postcard in the local shop
nor an outlaw with my likeness
nailed to every tree

I am a woman, Monsieur Lacan
of the feminine kind

and what I want to be, monsieur
is *loved* – not by you, but
by anyone else but you. . .

never trust a man. . .

never trust a man with a tiny goatee beard
a velvet voice and eyes that smoulder
hot as coals when you're in the dark

if he takes you back to his
ask for every key to every door to every room
and if you find in one
his last wife's dresses, shoes
the ashes of her worn-out dreams
and if he tells you that she travels light, left
in an unholy rush – what was he to do –
look closer girl and check
she didn't leave
without her body too

then bring to mind the ancient tale
of bluebeard and the women
that he wooed and wed

and if you know what's good for you
refuse his offer of a comfy bed, get out fast,
or soon it might be your ghost gathering dust
in the dingy back room of his past.

bonsai

she is neatly potted
in the home he has provided

each day he tends her
nourishes her
but not too richly – she
must not grow too strong

sometimes he sits her in the sun
but if she pushes shoots
in shapes he does not like
he quickly nips and clips them back

from time to time he twists her limbs with wire
and as he does he sprinkles her
with words of love

when friends come round
he smiles as they admire
his beautiful creation

why I do not take your advice

safe as houses, you said

ignoring the treachery
of the table corner that juts
the door handle that grabs
the rug that trips
the slate that slips

postcards from a cold country

snowflake

snowflake on my tongue
cold white kiss
tumbled from heaven

how easily you melt
my indifference

spider web

dew-laden at dawn
shimmering between haw twigs
a cradle for new-born dreams

heron

ungainly origami
of scrawn, feather, bone

the wind's fingers fold you
send you flapping

none for sorrow

magpie on a sheet of snow
hieroglyph of sorrow

I close my eyes, you are gone

the white page waits
the black ink flows

february on flanders moss

in morning sunshine
feathers black as mourning silk
death perches on a leafless tree

wraithed in mists, dark firs wait
like forgotten Roman armies
doomed to haunt the edge of time

a scots pine, stunted, stands
its branches gnarled as an ancient's hands
begging kindness from the passing clouds

in a flat green field, ditched around with brown
a scarecrow leans, the next along lies
face-down in the mud, nameless
soldier in the Somme

a shot rings out, twenty herons lift
into a sky of gun-metal grey
forty wings in a flap

late evening sun slants, the moss
beneath my feet makes
human gurgling sounds

behind my back my shadow draws
a silent ghost

there can be no staying here

By the ice-bound loch we walked
our feet scrunching virgin snows, casting
echoes in the still pool of the dusk.

A deer, startled by the noise
as we drew near darted off
between dark trunks of firs
elusive as a dream.

Where the old bridge heaves
its stony back over the flow of time
we stood and watched crazed
waters dash in swirls and whorls
with no beginnings and no ends.

We were mesmerised by the magic
of those liquid runes, the low laugh
in the river's throat
and would have stayed all night
but the wind came tugging at our coats
and woke us from that trance.

And then we understood –
there can be no staying here
between the old year and the new.

But still we stood, caught
on the hook of history,
our breath white in the freezing air,
trying to hold that moment, as if
in living cells, in human memory
we could preserve the ending of a century.

Then darkness swallowed up the sky.
The hand of time had drawn
a blind down on the dying year.

And in the deepest darkness of that death,
carried on the old year's final breath
we heard the newborn's mewling cry.

loose woman song

Don't break my toes and bind my feet
to mark my femininity –
I'd rather have feet big enough to kick
against such sad misogyny.

Don't truss me in a bible-belt
of narrow-minded chastity.
Don't lace me in a corset of dutiful conformity.

Don't weigh me down with golden rings,
don't chain me to the kitchen sink
I've a brain that needs to think -
so keep your drudgery.

Don't make me wear my hair tied tight
but let its wildness flow.
Don't veil my face and hide my light,
my fire, my spark, my glow.

Don't hem me in with prejudice
but let me breathe and grow
strong and graceful as a swan
wise as the moon, free as the wind.

Mother and Son

You stoop, lift a fresh-washed towel, pin it
to the drying rope. As in a silent dance,
you, your mother, bend, stretch, rise.

On your right, the fuschia bush
planted when you were a child
drips with red and purple buds.
High above clouds white and frothed as suds
scud across the blue sheet of the skies.

Once in this garden you ran wild,
once you dreamed below the bramley tree,
once you fought and played while Rosie
from the kitchen window watched and smiled.

No child upon it now, the old swing sways
an ancient creaking pendulum -
it ticks away the days since
you have swung from boy to man
who helps his mother hang the washing out

while from the kitchen window
another woman holds you in her gaze.

January's Child

I find him wedged between Lectures and Meetings,
Driving Courses, Deaths, Birthday Greetings,
with flattened hair, a gap-toothed smile
squatting cross-legged on his brief profile:
cheerful, excitable, eager to please, needs
love, stability, security. Name is Neil. Neil needs a family.

In the home he gobbles Corn Flakes, gets
ticked off for wanting too much sugar, gets
flicked off for wanting too much love. He
stares out at the winter wood, dreams about a
special tree with branches that can hug and hold.

I hope he never sees this morning's paper
where he is reduced from three foot six
to a few column inches, an out-of-focus photograph.
Gawky in t-shirt and shorts, eager to please
the stranger with the fancy camera, too excited
to sit too long at peace, he squints at the lens,
the camera clicks, January's child runs off.

zimmer warrior

she wields it with precision –
shove past her in a queue
this Boudicca will target your Achilles
and never miss

old lady

she limps
but will not use a stick

she has not lived this long, she says
to be a tripod

zimmer love

her constant companion
since her man passed on

and, she says, a twinkle in her eye
it never grumps or farts

old trees

with all their gnarls

and wrinkled barks

boast deeper roots

life after death

last night's storm has blown
a leafless tree across the burn

children leave the swings and chutes
the brightly coloured climbing frames

in death the tree blossoms
with laughing children

war widow

She sits alone in her darkened room,
curtains drawn against the blazing sun.
She does not hear the knocking at the door
the intermittent bleating of the phone.

In her hand she clasps the video's
remote control, finger trigger-ready
as miles of archive footage roll
to celebrate D-day and Victory.

Upstairs, buried in a mothballed-drawer
with war-time letters bound with silk,
a diamond ring we've never seen her wear,
a telegram grows yellow at the edges:
Lost in action. Normandy. 6th June, 1944.

Downstairs in the airless gloom
men in uniform and flickering monochrome,
turn to brave the camera lens,
give a smile, a wave, a nervous glance
then hurry off to waiting boats and planes.

She scans the screen. From time to time
she pushes on RECORD. Later, she rewinds
and checks each face, each smile once more.

We hush the children when we call;
she's bunkered in her loneliness,
locked into nineteen forty-four and we
are unborn strangers she has yet to meet.

Outside, in the summer heat
it is our turn to fret and wait
as forty years of buried grief,
unstable as an unexploded bomb,
threaten to detonate.

grief

You carry it for weeks
like a father carrying a hurt child
through a dark forest.

Lost in darkness
you hear the child whimper
you feel him grip you tight.

But open your eyes!
The child you carry has already healed,
the whimpering is your own.

Let the child go
set him on the forest floor
let him run off.

Then look up through the dark
you thought was solid as a slab of rock.

Even in the thickest forest
light filters through
when the blackest hour is past.

too late

at the cemetery
I hear you whisper, briefly,
to my father

such a tenderness
in the granite of your voice
something approaching love. . .

later we drive in silence
a mother, a daughter
grieving all we have lost

and I wonder – if I died
and lay beneath the soil

would you speak to me
in such gentle tones?

surviving the wreck

The sea swallowed me, then a dark
I thought must be the final one. Suddenly,
all around, ink-black seals, nudging
with curious snouts. Then him, scooping me
in his arms – still I recall his sea-green
selkie eyes in so much black.

A rush of white and I gulp the night,
gulping fit to burst the tender tissue of my heart.

Then I hear her voice. Such a small still voice.
And my legs kick, kick at the cold sea
that would pluck the life from me
and he now swimming by my side
eyes willing me to fight the tide
and my hands, finger to finger,
finger to thumb, grow skin
and my legs are a fishtail
strong, thrashing.

my skull is a shell
stolen from the ocean bed –
hear my daughter's voice
deep in its pearly whorl
a bubble of sweet air
keeping me abreast the swell. . .

He's smiling now, his teeth like
perfect pearls – oh I could let him
drown me in the emerald of his eyes.

But see, he's pointing to the shore
and a string of lights, draped like diamonds
on the dark breast of the hill. And I no longer
see his eyes, but the town, the house, the bed
where my child lies, tossing, writhing,
calling, calling as though she's drowning
in her dreams.

Grit and gravel scrape breasts, knuckles, knees.
I scrabble from the salt waves' sting,
lie lifeless as a washed-up jellyfish
but for the sobs which rise and fall
with the suck and rush of sea on shingle shore.
Dry arms scoop me up, blue eyes stare.
I know my child dreams peacefully once more.

Now each night I drown
in a deep ocean of sleep.

Waking with the dawn I carefully
fold back the crushed white sheet,
touch my soft-skinned thighs, my feet,
stretch my unwebbed fingers wide
and weep salt tears.

breaking free

shrouded in leaves you lie
beneath the sheltering trees

a half-hatched fledgling
in a cradle of jagged shell

claws curled around emptiness
black nib beak glued shut

eyes bulged beneath unopened lids
tiny wings half-formed

and I know that your fate might
so easily have been my own

the thrill of flight unrealised,
the song stillborn on a shrivelled tongue

ad for a muse

must be male, but not too masculine
must be prepared to sit statue still
hold his wheesht until I ask for inspiration

must be easy on the eye, not try to interfere
when I would rather be relaxing

must make a decent latte, have an over-developed
sensibility, an under-developed ego and preferably a very
large vocabulary   (gsoh a distinct advantage)

must not grind his teeth, fart, snort, snore or bore

professional rates/minimum holidays
luxuriant live-in accommodation
in the back-room of my brain

no references required
apply within

graffiti in red lipstick

sitting on this train, speeding
forwards, thinking back
to moments left behind
along this shining track
my head rattles with seeds of poetry

like jack's magic beans
metaphors take root in the dark tilth
of my brain, sprout eager shoots that strain
towards the light. I search my bag
for paper, pen, find none

my hand locates a lipstick – red -
the vinyl seats in front invite

I write . . .